IMPEACHMENT

IMPEACHMENT

DONALD TRUMP
AND THE HISTORY OF
PRESIDENTS IN PERIL

JAMES ROLAND

LERNER PUBLICATIONS ◆ MINNEAPOLIS

Lerner Publications Company
An imprint of Lerner Publishing Group, Inc.
241 First Avenue North
Minneapolis, MN 55401 USA

For reading levels and more information, look up this title at www.lernerbooks.com.

Main body text set in Rotis Serif Std 55 Regular. Typeface provided by Adobe Systems.

Editor: Alison Lorenz **Designer:** Martha Kranes

Library of Congress Cataloging-in-Publication Data

Names: Roland, James, author.
Title: Impeachment : Donald Trump and the history of presidents in peril / James Roland.
Description: Minneapolis : Lerner Publications, 2021 | Series: Gateway biographies | Includes
   bibliographical references and index. | Audience: Ages 9–14 | Audience: Grades 4–6 |
   Summary: "This issue biography offers an overview and history of the impeachment process,
   explores key players and moments in President Trump's impeachment, and explains the
   historic event's resolution"– Provided by publisher.
Identifiers: LCCN 2020004908 (print) | LCCN 2020004909 (ebook) | ISBN 9781728416175
   (library binding) | ISBN 9781728416199 (ebook)
Subjects: LCSH: Trump, Donald, 1946-–Impeachment–Juvenile literature. | Impeachments–
   United States–Juvenile literature.
Classification: LCC KF5076.T78 R65 2021 (print) | LCC KF5076.T78 (ebook) | DDC 973.933092–
   dc23

LC record available at https://lccn.loc.gov/2020004908
LC ebook record available at https://lccn.loc.gov/2020004909

Manufactured in the United States of America
1-48778-49187-4/17/2020

CONTENTS

President Donald Trump takes a phone call in the Oval Office in 2017.

On July 25, 2019, in the middle of a steamy Washington, DC, summer, the White House arranged a phone call. President Donald Trump would congratulate Volodymyr Zelensky on being elected president of Ukraine just a few months earlier. After some small talk, Zelensky said that his country was ready to buy more missiles from the United States. The missiles would help defend Ukraine in its ongoing war with Russia.

Trump responded, "I would like you to do us a favor, though, because our country has been through a lot and Ukraine knows a lot about it." He mentioned a company called CrowdStrike. Trump suggested the company may have meddled in the 2016 US presidential election. The story was part of a popular but false conspiracy theory. Some claimed CrowdStrike was a Ukrainian company that hacked the computers of the Democratic National Committee during the campaign. But US intelligence agencies such as the FBI and CIA agreed that Russia

President Volodymyr Zelensky of Ukraine in 2020

was responsible for the hack. The agencies had evidence that Russia, not Ukraine, had tried to sway the election. CrowdStrike was a California-based cybersecurity company Democrats had hired to look into the hack.

More significantly, Trump urged Zelensky to look into former US vice president Joe Biden's son Hunter. From 2014 to 2019, Hunter Biden had sat on the board of directors of a Ukrainian energy company called Burisma Holdings. From January 2009 to 2017, Joe Biden had been President Barack Obama's vice president. Biden was one of the administration's leaders on Ukraine policy.

Trump implied that it was corrupt for Biden's son to hold the position. The company had been the subject of criminal investigations in the past. But no one had found evidence that Hunter Biden had done anything wrong.

For much of 2019, Joe Biden was seen as a likely Democratic presidential nominee. Many thought he would face Trump, a Republican, in the 2020 election. Democrats and others, therefore, viewed Trump's mention of Hunter Biden on the phone call as politically motivated.

President Barack Obama (*right*) and Vice President Joe Biden in 2016

If voters thought Hunter had profited unfairly from his father's vice presidency, they might be less likely to vote for the elder Biden. Trump claimed he had brought up Hunter Biden because he was worried about corruption in Ukraine. But Democrats saw it as an attempt to seek the help of a foreign country to win the 2020 election.

Earlier in the summer, the White House had ordered a hold on nearly $400 million in congressionally approved military aid to Ukraine. In light of this, the requests he made of Zelensky on the July 25 phone call took on a new weight. It appeared to many that Trump had made a dangerous suggestion. If Zelensky did not investigate

Something of Value

Candidates need a lot of money and support to run for office. But federal election laws decide who can contribute to campaigns. Candidates can't receive money or anything else of value from foreign countries. This law came up many times during Trump's impeachment. Democrats argued that asking the Ukrainian president to investigate a political rival was the same as asking for something of value. This would mean the president had broken the law.

Hunter Biden, Ukraine would not receive the military aid it needed to defend itself against Russia.

The phone call lasted only about thirty minutes. But that half hour would trigger months of political infighting, public protests, and a set of hearings that gripped the nation. It would also make Donald Trump only the third president in US history to be impeached.

WHAT DOES IMPEACHMENT MEAN?

Impeachment is the way Congress can charge presidents with misconduct and even remove them from office. A president doesn't have to commit a crime to be impeached. Presidents can break their oath of office in ways that aren't necessarily crimes. Impeachment is one way to address these actions.

Three impeachable offenses are described in the Constitution: treason, bribery, and high crimes and misdemeanors. Treason means to help an enemy of the US during wartime. Bribery occurs when public officials make an exchange that benefits them personally rather than benefiting the public good.

But what exactly are high crimes and misdemeanors? They include presidential misconduct that isn't treason or bribery. The country's founders purposely left the definition of high crimes and misdemeanors vague in the Constitution. This is because no one could foresee all the ways a president might break the oath of office.

They debated whether to include impeachment in the Constitution. Eventually, most of them decided that a president shouldn't be untouchable as a king or queen was. As a coequal branch of government, Congress can check presidential power.

Congress makes up the legislative branch—the House of Representatives and the Senate. It's responsible for creating or changing laws. It also creates an annual government budget. The president is the head of the executive branch and has the power to enforce the laws. The president must also sign off on government spending. The judicial branch includes the Supreme Court and other government courts. Courts are responsible for interpreting laws. All three branches are related in a system of checks and balances. Presidents, for example, can veto laws or items in the budget. Congress has the power to override vetoes. The Supreme Court can make decisions about the constitutionality of laws or policies. The court's rulings then become law.

Impeachment is a rarely used check on presidential power. It has two parts. First, the House of Representatives brings charges against the president. These charges are known as articles of impeachment. Once the House approves the charges, they are sent to the Senate. The Senate sets up an impeachment trial. Senators serve as jurors while the chief justice of the Supreme Court oversees. The Senate can vote to acquit the president, or clear the charges. But if the Senate convicts the president, the president must leave office. Conviction requires a vote of two-thirds of the Senate to pass. If a president is convicted and removed from office, the vice president is sworn in as president.

Only three presidents have been impeached. Before Trump, Andrew Johnson and Bill Clinton were impeached

If Not Impeachment, Then What?

Impeachment is the most serious way Congress can express disapproval of a president's actions. Another way is censure. A censure is a formal statement of disapproval. It must be approved by a majority of the Senate. The only successful one happened in 1834. The Senate censured President Andrew Jackson when he closed the federal bank. The House tried twice to censure Trump. But neither effort got enough support.

by the House. But, like Trump, neither was removed from office by the Senate.

Johnson faced eleven articles of impeachment after months of buildup. Johnson had become president after Abraham Lincoln's death. But he often clashed with Congress during his presidency. After the Civil War ended, many lawmakers wanted to give freed slaves more rights. Johnson disagreed and vetoed new laws that aimed to do so. Then Johnson fired his secretary of war. The House claimed the firing was illegal and impeached him. The Senate vote fell one short of removing Johnson from office.

Clinton was impeached after lying about his inappropriate relationship with an intern at the White House. Clinton had encouraged the woman to deny that they had ever had an affair. The House charged him

President Andrew Johnson (*right*) receives notice of his impeachment in 1868.

Independent Counsel Ken Starr testifies during Clinton's impeachment hearings in 1998.

with lying under oath and obstruction of justice. But the Senate did not come close to a two-thirds majority to convict him.

President Richard Nixon came close to being impeached as a result of the Watergate scandal. In 1972 people working on Nixon's reelection campaign broke into the Democratic Party headquarters. They were trying to find information they could use against the Democrats. At first, Nixon denied knowledge of the break-in. Later, though, evidence showed he had been involved and tried to cover it up. The House Judiciary Committee drafted three articles of impeachment soon after. Before the full House of Representatives could vote on them, Nixon resigned. He was the first president to willingly leave office.

Watergate

The Watergate scandal caused Nixon to resign the presidency in 1974. The scandal was named for the Watergate complex in Washington, DC. Nixon supporters broke into the complex to reach the Democratic headquarters. But the break-in at Watergate was only the start of Nixon's troubles. The investigation into the break-in revealed many other crimes. Nixon's staff had improperly spied, misused taxpayer money, sabotaged rival campaigns, and more.

Nixon announces his resignation in 1974.

Trump used press conferences and other media events to make the case for his innocence.

If Trump ever considered resigning, he never said so publicly. Instead, he used impeachment as a rallying cry. He claimed Democrats were plotting against him. The president often used Twitter to argue his innocence. He also claimed the impeachment process was unfair.

THE ROAD TO IMPEACHMENT

Critics had long accused Trump of impeachable acts. They said Trump was improperly profiting from foreign leaders who stayed at hotels and resorts he owned. The Constitution doesn't allow presidents to take payments from foreign leaders. This is because leaders may be trying to bribe the president. Critics also objected to

Trump's abrasive style and divisive policies. Yet the most serious objection Trump's critics raised was that he may have sought Russia's help to get elected in 2016.

The FBI and CIA discovered that Russia had hacked computers belonging to the Democratic National Committee in 2016. But they weren't sure the Russians had done this independently. The FBI needed to find out if the Russians were working with the Trump campaign. It is illegal for US political campaigns to get foreign help.

The FBI looked into contacts between Russians and members of Trump's campaign. Among those under scrutiny was Trump's national security adviser, retired general Michael Flynn. The FBI investigated Flynn for suspicious contacts with the Russian ambassador. They also investigated paid work he had done for other foreign countries.

Just a few months after taking office, Trump fired FBI director James Comey. Trump claimed the firing was based on how Comey had handled an investigation into Hillary Clinton, Trump's 2016 Democratic opponent. But Comey later confirmed that in February 2017, Trump had encouraged him to drop the FBI's investigation into Flynn. To many, it appeared that Trump was trying to interfere with an FBI investigation. This could be an obstruction of justice.

In the spring of 2017, former FBI director Robert Mueller was appointed as a special counsel. Mueller would oversee an investigation into Russian involvement in the 2016 election.

Two years later, Mueller finished his investigation and released a report. The report did not establish that Trump's campaign had actively worked with Russia. But it did list instances where Trump and his administration possibly obstructed Mueller's investigation and other investigations. Department of Justice guidelines said that a sitting president couldn't be indicted for a crime. Therefore, no charges were brought against Trump. The report noted that, instead, Congress would have to address possible obstruction charges.

Many members of Congress believed that the Mueller report was enough to launch impeachment hearings. The House Judiciary Committee and the House Intelligence Committee heard from Mueller that summer. But Mueller didn't make any major new accusations or announce charges against Trump.

The president and his allies declared themselves innocent. They tried to frame Mueller's appearance in Congress as the end of the investigation and a moment of victory. But for Trump's critics, the Mueller investigation would soon be relevant again. They thought Trump had received foreign help in 2016. This made the accusation that he had tried to do so in 2019 all the more believable.

SHAPING THE STORY

On July 24, 2019, Mueller told members of Congress that Russia had interfered with the 2016 election to Trump's

"The Russian government interfered in the 2016 presidential election in sweeping and systematic fashion."

Mueller Report: Page 1, Volume I

Hon. Robert S. Mueller, III

Special Counsel Robert Mueller speaks to the House Judiciary Committee in July 2019.

benefit. The next day, Trump made his call to Zelensky. Without Trump realizing it, that thirty-minute call moved him closer to impeachment than the Mueller investigation ever did.

Events in the first half of 2019 shaped the story around impeachment. In the spring, former vice president Joe Biden made an announcement. He would seek the Democratic Party nomination for president in the 2020 election.

Around then one of Trump's personal lawyers, Rudy Giuliani, started giving interviews that raised questions

Rudy Giuliani

about the Bidens. There was no evidence that Hunter Biden had done anything wrong in his position at Burisma. Still, Trump, Giuliani, and other Republicans seized upon the Biden connection. They tried to tie the Bidens into larger concerns about corruption in Ukraine.

Members of Congress were leaving Washington, DC, for their summer recess. Some guessed that the question of impeachment as it related to the Mueller investigation would be addressed when they returned in the fall. Trump's phone call with Zelensky had not yet been made public.

Back in their home districts, lawmakers held town halls. They heard from their constituents about Trump and other issues of the day. Meanwhile, events unfolded in the White House that would lead to a historic end to 2019.

THE INQUIRY BEGINS

The public might never have learned of Trump's call with Zelensky. But someone in the administration learned of the discussion and sent letters to the chairs of the House and Senate Intelligence Committees. The letter writer was a whistleblower—someone who reports on suspected wrongdoing from within an organization.

The House committee chair was Representative Adam Schiff of California. Members of his staff directed the whistleblower to report the same concerns to the intelligence community's inspector general. The inspector was responsible for investigating problems or possible misconduct within the community.

The whistleblower's complaint remained out of public view for several more weeks. Meanwhile, the online political magazine *Politico* reported that the White House had ordered a hold on military aid to Ukraine. The article noted that members of Congress were concerned.

Whistleblowers

The identity of the whistleblower remains secret. Many believe that whistleblowers should be able to stay anonymous. This way their careers, families, and safety are protected. If their identities could be revealed, whistleblowers may be too afraid to come forward. That's why certain laws exist to keep whistleblowers' names hidden.

The White House claimed the hold was put in place to make sure the money was being spent with US national interests in mind. The White House also said that other countries in Europe were not providing Ukraine with enough support.

With little fanfare, the US finally released the assistance to Ukraine on September 11. The matter of the aid had not attracted much attention over the summer. Then, on September 20, the *Wall Street Journal* published a story linking the hold on the $391 million in military aid and Trump's request that Zelensky investigate the Bidens. Almost immediately, Republicans and Democrats disagreed about what had taken place and how to interpret it. Republicans argued that the whistleblower hadn't actually been in on the call, so the accusations were just hearsay. Democrats said the whistleblower's account and the delay in aiding vulnerable Ukraine needed further investigation. On September 24, Speaker of the House Nancy Pelosi announced that the House would begin a formal impeachment inquiry.

Aiming to put the controversy to rest, the White House released a summary of the phone call. Trump claimed the summary showed he had done nothing wrong. But the summary proved that he had asked Zelensky to investigate the Bidens. Many saw Trump's request as an appeal for Ukraine to get involved in US politics. Trump emphasized his focus on the Bidens during a press conference on October 3. He urged China to investigate the Bidens and stated again his hope that Zelensky would do so.

Nancy Pelosi answers questions after announcing the House's impeachment inquiry in September 2019.

If anything, the White House phone call summary and Trump's comments supported the Democrats' argument. They seemed to strengthen the idea that Trump was pressuring an ally to try to influence the 2020 presidential election. Within two weeks, the House Intelligence Committee began questioning members of Trump's administration. But the White House announced early on it would not cooperate.

QUID PRO QUO?

In the weeks after the whistleblower's complaint went public, many began using a Latin phrase to describe the scandal. They claimed the military aid delay, as well as

Trump and Zelensky at the United Nations in September 2019

a meeting the White House had promised Zelensky, were part of a quid pro quo. The phrase translates as "this for that." It means the exchange of a thing or service for something of value. Often the exchange may not be legal or ethical.

In the Ukraine scandal, the quid pro quo was having Zelensky launch investigations into the Bidens and CrowdStrike in order to receive nearly $400 million in US military aid. At the United Nations on September 25, Trump and Zelensky appeared together. Trump again denied doing anything inappropriate. Zelensky said he felt no pressure from the president. But some noted that the Ukrainian president needed the US as an ally and couldn't afford to anger Trump. Possibly, Zelensky had no choice but to take Trump's side.

Republicans argued that the Bidens hadn't been investigated and Ukraine eventually received the aid. Therefore, no quid pro quo took place. They claimed Trump and his administration had done nothing wrong. Trump and his allies also repeatedly argued that asking Zelensky to investigate the Bidens showed the president wanted to fight corruption in Ukraine. Democrats countered that if Trump truly wanted to fight corruption, the Bidens would not have been the only targets he mentioned. And Trump would have taken other actions against corruption while in office.

In October Mick Mulvaney, the acting White House chief of staff, seemed to reveal the truth about the quid

Joe Biden (*right*) and his son Hunter

pro quo. During a press conference, he acknowledged that Trump wanted Ukraine to agree to the investigations before he released the military aid. "Get over it," Mulvaney said. "There's going to be political influence in foreign policy." Finally, he added, "Elections have consequences."

HEARINGS AND IMPEACHMENT

Mulvaney later tried to walk back his comments. But his words were captured on video and heard by a room full of reporters. On November 13, the House Intelligence Committee impeachment hearings began. Schiff referenced Mulvaney's remarks as he summed up the charges to be discussed. "Must we simply 'get over it?'" asked Schiff. "If this is not impeachable conduct, what is? Does the oath of office itself . . . still have meaning?"

Over the next week, twelve witnesses took questions from Democratic and Republican lawmakers. Both parties also had lawyers to question the witnesses. As the hearings went on, several striking moments took place. Gordon Sondland, the US ambassador to the European Union, said a quid pro quo was definitely in place. Trump would give Zelensky military aid and a White House meeting in exchange for an investigation, or at least the announcement of an investigation, into Burisma and the 2016 election meddling. "Everyone was in the loop," Sondland added. His remark implied that other top members of Trump's staff were also involved.

Another witness was Fiona Hill, formerly a top Russia adviser to the White House. Hill made it clear that Sondland, Giuliani, and others involved in the Ukraine scandal had their own political goals. They were not

Gordon Sondland testified that a quid pro quo existed between Trump and Zelensky during his November 2019 hearing.

Fiona Hill testifies to the House Intelligence Committee in November 2019.

focused on the security of Ukraine, Europe, or the US. Sondland, Hill suggested, had been directed to pursue "a domestic political errand." Meanwhile, she and her staff were "involved in national security foreign policy. And those two things had just diverged."

Having dismissed the last witness, Schiff concluded that "there is nothing more dangerous than an unethical president who believes he is above the law. We are better than that." With that, he ended the hearing.

The action moved next to the House Judiciary Committee, led by Representative Jerry Nadler of New York. The Judiciary Committee decided not to invite more witnesses from Trump's administration. Instead, they called four constitutional law scholars to review the evidence already presented. The scholars would consider whether Trump's actions were impeachable offenses.

Republicans called Professor Jonathan Turley to testify. Turley disagreed with Trump's claim that the call to Zelensky was faultless. But he criticized the evidence providing the basis for impeachment. "The current legal case for impeachment is not just woefully inadequate but in some respects dangerous as the basis for impeachment of an American president," he said. He added that this impeachment could set a precedent for future flimsy impeachment cases.

Professor Michael Gerhardt, whom the Democrats called, argued the opposite. He said the president's actions were definitely impeachable. Further, if the House didn't impeach Trump, it would damage Congress's ability to check future presidents. "If Congress fails to impeach here, then the impeachment process has lost all meaning and . . . our Constitution's carefully crafted safeguards against the establishment of a king on American soil," Gerhardt warned.

The Judiciary Committee hearing was over. A majority of House members agreed to approve two articles of impeachment: abuse of power and obstruction of Congress. The abuse charge related to accusations that Trump pressured Ukraine to investigate a political rival. The obstruction charge related to the White House's refusal to allow witnesses to testify or to provide documents requested by the House.

Many questioned why the articles of impeachment were so narrow. What about the examples of obstruction in the Mueller report or the possible constitutional violations? House Democrats believed that it would be simpler to make the case for limited articles of impeachment to the Senate and the public. It would also prevent Republicans from claiming that Democrats were throwing whatever they could at the president.

The House spent a long day on December 17 discussing the two articles of impeachment. Democrats and Republicans traded the same accusations they had for months. But as the hour grew late and the debate ended, the House decided not to take a vote. Lawmakers gathered again the next morning to give each article of impeachment a separate vote. On the abuse of power charge, the vote was 230–197 in favor. On the obstruction of Congress charge, the vote was 229–198. No Republicans

Nancy Pelosi (*center*) speaks after the House impeached Trump on December 18, 2019.

voted for either charge. Only a few Democrats strayed from their party's preference.

The first phase of impeachment ended right before the winter holidays. The House decided to wait until January to deliver the articles of impeachment to the Senate. The Senate was controlled by Republicans. Many of them strongly supported the president.

THE SENATE AND ACQUITTAL

At the start of 2020, the Senate took up its role in impeachment. Most people guessed the Senate would acquit Trump. But many questions were still unanswered. Many wondered whether any new information would come out. Some asked whether any Republicans would split with their party and vote to convict the president. Would impeachment affect how the Democrats chose their presidential nominee? Would impeachment—even one that ended with acquittal—sway any voters in November?

On January 15 Pelosi named seven impeachment managers. The managers would act as prosecutors in the Senate trial. Schiff and Nadler were among them. That day the articles of impeachment were delivered to the Senate.

On January 16 the Senate convened for the third time in its history to consider articles of impeachment against a president. The Senate swore in Chief Justice John Roberts to oversee the trial. Senators took an oath

Mitch McConnell speaks during the Senate's impeachment trial in January 2020.

to be fair and impartial jurors. But before the trial began, Senate majority leader Mitch McConnell appeared on TV. He admitted he would not be impartial. "Everything I do during this, I'm coordinating with the White House counsel," he said. "There will be no difference between the president's position and our position as to how to handle this."

The comment alarmed Democrats and constitutional scholars. They complained that the Senate is meant to be an unbiased jury. Though impeachment is a political process, the expectation was that Democrats and Republicans alike would treat it seriously.

On January 21 the House began to make its case against the president. Senate Republicans refused to allow the Democrats to call witnesses. They also decided against requesting documents from the White House to present as evidence.

The House managers argued that letting Trump remain in office would send a signal. Future presidents might think that abusing the power of the presidency was acceptable. The managers warned that the fairness of the next election was at stake. They argued that the trial itself was a sham unless Republicans allowed witnesses and evidence to be examined.

Trump's defense team took over on January 25. They argued that the House had failed to provide direct evidence of the quid pro quo. The House's case, they claimed, was built on speculation and secondhand accounts. Impeachment was the Democrats' attempt to "steal" the 2020 election. The defense also suggested that the Bidens' actions were indeed suspicious. Asking Ukraine to investigate was the only way to address them.

The senators questioned the House managers and Trump's defense team. But by the end of the trial, very

Party Lines

Because Clinton's impeachment happened only about twenty years before Trump's, many compared the two. Clinton, a Democrat, had the support of his party during impeachment. But unlike Trump, Clinton also had members of the other party supporting him. Five Republican senators joined Democrats in voting to acquit Clinton's obstruction charge. Ten voted with Democrats to acquit the charge of lying under oath.

BREAKING NEWS GUILTY 47 NOT GUILTY 53
PRESIDENT TRUMP NOT GUILTY ON BOTH ARTICLES OF IMPEACHMENT

SENATE VOTE	34 VOTES NEEDED TO ACQUIT	ARTICLE II: OBSTRUCTION OF CONGRESS		CNN
		53 NOT GUILTY	47 GUILTY	NAS ▲ 40.71

THE IMPEACHMENT TRIAL OF DONALD J. TRUMP   THE LEAD

Senate Floor
Capitol Hill
4:33 PM ET

Major news networks broadcast the results of Trump's impeachment trial.

little new information had come out. It was time for senators to vote.

On the abuse of power charge, the motion to convict failed 48–52. The obstruction of Congress charge failed 47–53. Republican senator Mitt Romney was the only one of his party to vote for conviction, on the charge of abuse of power. Immediately, Trump and his supporters criticized Romney. They suggested he leave the Republican Party.

In the hours after the trial ended, senators from each party expressed very different views. Republicans stressed the importance of moving on from impeachment to address other issues. Democrats regretted that so few of their colleagues had come out against the president's actions.

AFTER IMPEACHMENT

Trump was the first president to run for reelection after being impeached. Clinton was impeached in his second term. He didn't have to consider how it would affect his chances of reelection. Johnson took office in 1865 after Abraham Lincoln's death. He wanted to be the Democratic nominee in the 1868 election. But he lost the party's nomination in July 1868. The Watergate scandal began in the months leading up to Nixon's reelection in 1972. But investigations and hearings didn't start until 1973. They continued until his resignation halfway through his second term.

Visitors stand outside the White House in the hours before Nixon's resignation.

Impeachment and Public Opinion

Public opinion polls give an idea of how people feel about the president at a certain time. It may seem odd that Trump said impeachment would make him more popular. But history in part supported the claim. When Clinton admitted to his affair, his approval rating was about 60 percent. By the week he was impeached, it had jumped to 71 percent. Nixon's approval ratings told a different story. They fell from around 50 percent when Watergate hearings began to 24 percent when Nixon resigned.

Nixon eventually lost the support of most Republicans in Congress and many Republican voters. But Trump kept the enthusiastic support of his party through the impeachment hearings, trial, and beyond.

Trump's reelection campaign used his impeachment to generate support and donations. Campaign officials said the impeachment was a sign that Democrats weren't being fair or responsible leaders. They framed Trump as a victim who needed his supporters to rally around him.

In speeches around the country, Trump maintained his innocence. He openly criticized and insulted Democrats such as Adam Schiff and Nancy Pelosi. His supporters cheered him on at these rallies. Democrats warned that the acquittal would only make the president more likely to abuse the power of his office again.

Trump speaks at a rally in New Hampshire soon after being acquitted in 2020.

Trump's impeachment raised questions about the relationship between Congress and the president. Many Republicans warned Democrats against pushing ahead with impeachment. Republicans said Democrats could expect the next Democratic president to be impeached by a Republican House. "From here on out, most presidents will now get impeached when the opposite party holds the House," former White House chief of staff Reince Priebus said after Trump's impeachment. "This is a new political game that will play out for decades to come."

Schiff saw things differently. The White House had blocked many people from testifying and refused to turn over documents requested by the House. Schiff argued that through these actions, Trump may have set a precedent Republicans will regret later on. "If they're prepared to [accept] this, they must be willing to accept the fact that when there's a Democratic president that they believe is engaged in any kind of misconduct, they will be powerless to find out," Schiff said.

Protesters called for Trump's removal as his impeachment trial was underway.

Trump supporters held a counterprotest during an impeachment rally in New York City.

The ways in which the Trump impeachment will affect national politics in the years ahead are hard to predict. Trump's impeachment could signal a new era in which impeachment becomes common. The divide between Republicans and Democrats could grow wider. Or perhaps it will inspire citizens to reflect on what they want from their elected leaders. Perhaps the impeachment will result in calls for greater unity. Regardless of how the political landscape changes, one thing is certain: the Trump impeachment will be talked about, studied, and debated for many years to come.

IMPORTANT DATES

February 24, 1868	The House of Representatives votes to impeach President Andrew Johnson.
August 8, 1974	Richard Nixon becomes the first president to resign from office.
December 19, 1998	President Bill Clinton is impeached on charges of lying under oath and obstructing Congress.
November 8, 2016	Donald Trump is elected the forty-fifth president of the United States.
February 15, 2019	Trump signs a spending bill that includes $141 million for Ukraine's security needs, adding to $250 million promised earlier.
April 25, 2019	Former vice president Joe Biden announces his candidacy for president of the United States.
July 18, 2019	White House officials announce to other agencies in the administration that a hold has been placed on the nearly $400 million in military aid to Ukraine.
July 25, 2019	Trump calls Zelensky and asks him to investigate the Bidens and possible Ukrainian involvement in the 2016 US presidential election.

August 12, 2019	A whistleblower files a complaint suggesting that Trump may have improperly pressured Ukraine to interfere in the 2020 election.
September 11, 2019	The aid to Ukraine is released. The White House provides no explanation about the hold or the sudden release.
September 24, 2019	Speaker of the House Nancy Pelosi announces a formal impeachment inquiry.
November 13, 2019	The House Intelligence Committee opens impeachment hearings.
December 13, 2019	The House Judiciary Committee votes to approve two articles of impeachment, charging the president with abuse of power and obstruction of Congress.
December 18, 2019	The House of Representatives votes in favor of both articles of impeachment. Trump becomes the third president to be impeached.
January 16, 2020	The Senate convenes for the start of Trump's impeachment trial.
February 5, 2020	The Senate votes to acquit Trump of both articles of impeachment.

SOURCE NOTES

7   "Letter from President Donald J. Trump to the Speaker of the House of Representatives," White House, December 17, 2019, https://www.whitehouse.gov/briefings-statements/letter -president-donald-j-trump-speaker-house-representatives/.

26 Jessica Taylor, "'Get Over It': Politics Is Part of Foreign Policy, Mulvaney Says," NPR, October 17, 2019, https://www.npr.org /2019/10/17/770979659/watch-white-house-holds-now-rare -press-briefing-amid-impeachment-syria-conflicts.

26 "READ: Adam Schiff's Opening Statement in First Public Impeachment Hearing," *U.S. News & World Report*, November 13, 2019, https://www.usnews.com/news/politics/articles /2019-11-13/read-adam-schiffs-opening-statement-in-first -public-impeachment-hearing.

27 Marshall Cohen, Ellie Kaufman, and Lauren Fox, "Five Takeaways from Gordon Sondland's Bombshell Testimony," CNN, November 21, 2019, https://www.cnn.com/2019/11/20/politics /gordon-sondland-hearing-takeaways/index.html.

28 Manu Raju and Jeremy Herb, "I Think This Is All Going to Blow Up: Witness Says EU Ambassador Was Running 'Domestic, Political Errand,'" CNN, November 21, 2019, https://www.cnn .com/2019/11/21/politics/fiona-hill-david-holmes-public -impeachment-hearing/index.html.

28 Philip Ewing and Brian Naylor, "Impeachment Hearings Wrap as Fiona Hill Slams GOP's 'Fictional' Ukraine Account," NPR, November 21, 2019, https://www.npr.org/2019/11/21/778657384 /what-to-watch-for-in-impeachment-hearing-with-fiona-hill -david-holmes.

29 Lynn Sweet, "Law Prof Jonathan Turley: GOP Witness at Trump Impeachment Hearing Raised on Chicago's North Side," *Chicago Sun-Times*, December 4, 2019, https://chicago.suntimes.com /columnists/2019/12/4/20996415/law-prof-jonathan-turley -witness-trump-impeachment-judiciary-hearing-raised-chicago -north-side.

29 Philip Ewing, "Judiciary Committee Takes Up Impeachment in Hearing with Legal Scholars," NPR, December 4, 2019, https:// www.npr.org/2019/12/04/784186196/judiciary-hearing-to-open -final-act-of-democrats-trump-impeachment-saga.

32 Grace Segers et al., "Judiciary Committee Ends Debate on Impeachment Articles," CBS News, December 13, 2019, https:// www.cbsnews.com/live-news/articles-of-impeachment-trump -house-judiciary-committee-hearing-markup-vote-live/.

37 Aaron Blake, "Analysis | Is Impeachment Suddenly Going to Be the New Normal? Eh," *Washington Post*, December 19, 2019, https://www.washingtonpost.com/politics/2019/12/19 /is-impeachment-suddenly-going-be-new-normal-eh/.

38 "Transcript: NPR's Follow-Up Interview with Rep. Adam Schiff on Impeachment Inquiry," NPR, December 3, 2019, https://www .npr.org/2019/12/03/784257412/transcript-nprs-follow-up -interview-with-rep-adam-schiff-on-impeachment-inquiry.

SELECTED BIBLIOGRAPHY

"Document: Read the Whistle-Blower Complaint." *New York Times*, September 26, 2019. https://www.nytimes.com/interactive /2019/09/26/us/politics/whistle-blower-complaint.html.

Gienger, Viola, and Ryan Goodman. "Timeline: Trump, Giuliani, Biden, and Ukrainegate (Updated)." Just Security. Last modified January 31, 2020. https://www.justsecurity.org/66271/timeline-trump-giuliani -bidens-and-ukrainegate/.

"Impeachment." US House of Representatives. Accessed February 19, 2020. https://history.house.gov/Institution/Origins-Development /Impeachment/.

Law, Tara. "What to Know about the US Presidents Who've Been Impeached." *Time*. Last modified February 5, 2020. https://time .com/5552679/impeached-presidents.

Mascaro, Lisa, and Mary Clarke Jalonick. "Trump Impeachment Inquiry." Associated Press, December 13, 2019. https://apnews.com /Trumpimpeachmentinquiry.

"*PBS News Hour:* Ukraine." PBS. Accessed February 19, 2020.
https://www.pbs.org/newshour/tag/ukraine.

"Stories about Ukraine." NPR. Accessed February 19, 2020. https://
www.npr.org/tags/126978660/ukraine.

"The Trump-Ukraine Impeachment Inquiry Report." December 2019.
Available online at Just Security. Accessed February 19, 2020.
https://www.justsecurity.org/wp-content/uploads/2019/12
/impeachment-report-majority-schiff-intelligence-december-3
-2019.pdf.

Wolf, Zachary B., and Curt Merrill. "How Trump's Impeachment Stacks
Up, in Four Charts." CNN, December 18, 2019. https://www.cnn
.com/2019/12/17/politics/impeachment-history-johnson-nixon
-clinton-trump/index.html.

FURTHER READING

BOOKS

Krasner, Barbara. *Exploring the Executive Branch*. Minneapolis: Lerner Publications, 2020.

Find out what presidents do, who helps them, and how they all work together.

Sherman, Jill. *Donald Trump: Outspoken Personality and President*. Minneapolis: Lerner Publications, 2017.

Read more about the forty-fifth president.

Smith-Llera, Danielle. *Exploring the Legislative Branch*. Minneapolis: Lerner Publications, 2020.

Discover who works in Congress, how representatives make laws, and the legislative branch's other duties.

WEBSITES

Ducksters: United States Government—The Constitution
https://www.ducksters.com/history/us_constitution.php

Learn the basics of the Constitution and the history behind its creation.

Kids in the House
https://kids-clerk.house.gov/grade-school/

Tour the Capitol, learn more about Congress's history, and find out how a bill becomes a law with this website from the House of Representatives.

TFK Explains: The Impeachment Process
https://www.timeforkids.com/g34/tfk-explains-impeachment-process-2/

Still confused about impeachment? Read this overview of the process.

INDEX

PHOTO ACKNOWLEDGMENTS

Image credits: Saul Loeb/AFP/Getty Images, pp. 2, 24; Jabin Botsford/The Washington Post/Getty Images, p. 6; Sven Hoppe/picture alliance/Getty Images, p. 8; Leigh Vogel/WireImage/Getty Images, p. 9; Everett Historical/Shutterstock.com, p. 13; Scott J. Ferrell/Congressional Quarterly/Getty Images, p. 14; Dirck Halstead/Liaison/Hulton Archive/Getty Images, p. 15; Mandel Ngan/AFP/Getty Images, p. 16; Jonathan Ernst/Pool/Getty Images, p. 19; Roy Rochlin/Getty Images, p. 20; Mark Wilson/Getty Images, p. 23; Teresa Kroeger/Getty Images, p. 25; Jim Watson/AFP/Getty Images, p. 26; Andrew Caballero-Reynolds/AFP/Getty Images, p. 27; Brendan Smialowski/AFP/Getty Images, p. 28; Ting Shen/Xinhua/Getty Images, p. 30; Senate Television/Getty Images, p. 32; Robert Alexander/Getty Images, p. 34; Bettmann/Getty Images, p. 35; Drew Angerer/Getty Images, p. 37; Aurora Samperio/NurPhoto/Getty Images, p. 38; Michael Brochstein/SOPA Images/LightRocket/Getty Images, p. 39.

Cover: Win McNamee/AFP/Getty Images; Win McNamee/Getty Images; Jesse Harrison Whitehurst/PhotoQuest/Getty Images.